Terms and Conditions

LEGAL NOTICE

The Publisher has strived to be as accurate and complete as possible in the creation of this report, notwithstanding the fact that he does not warrant or represent at any time that the contents within are accurate due to the rapidly changing nature of the Internet.

While all attempts have been made to verify information provided in this publication, the Publisher assumes no responsibility for errors, omissions, or contrary interpretation of the subject matter herein. Any perceived slights of specific persons, peoples, or organizations are unintentional.

In practical advice books, like anything else in life, there are no guarantees of income made. Readers are cautioned to reply on their own judgment about their individual circumstances to act accordingly.

This book is not intended for use as a source of legal, business, accounting or financial advice. All readers are advised to seek services of competent professionals in legal, business, accounting and finance fields.

You are encouraged to print this book for easy reading.

Table Of Contents

Foreword

Chapter 1:
What Is SEO

Chapter 2:
Intro to Indexing

Chapter 3:
What Your Page Needs For Indexing

Chapter 4:
The Indexing Procedure

Chapter 5:
From Google

Wrapping Up

Foreword

SEO? It's an acronym for Search Engine Optimization. But what SEO truly entails is making money on the net. I don't mean the act of putting up ad's and selling things online that you hope individuals will purchase.

What I do mean is making whatever you have available no matter if it has a price tag on it or not simply and readily available to the search engines. As you know individuals mostly utilize the Net to discover information. When somebody is attempting to discover information they tend to utilize a search engine.

When discussing SEO we have to look at the big picture or the whole pie. I'm going to explain to you how everything comes together for you when you're utilizing a search engine as either a surfer/searcher or a marketer/publisher.

Search Engine Optimization Strategies – Part 1

Chapter 1:
What Is SEO

Synopsis

There's a multimillion dollar industry of SEO "pros". Getting individuals into search engines or getting them in a higher place in the listings on a search engine is a business all on its own. If the chief idea behind getting traffic wasn't acquiring cash, there would be no such industry.

SEO is nothing more than a lot of tricks and hints and occasionally good sense that when utilized in the correct combination or alone will help you out in the Search Engines. You might learn a few fresh terms here or not know the terms I am utilizing but I'll explain and later on there's a whole section on it.

The Basics

A fast way to explain how you view results on a search engine results page or SERP is as follows. Search engines are much like adolescents. Adolescents "rank" individuals based on how popular they are and how much individuals pay attention to them. Search engines accomplish the same thing.

There are a 1000000 search engines but Google is the top and that's what we are going to be working with now. Everything I'm going to talk about here may be utilized for and with any search engine as each and every search engine is based on the same precepts.

In order to comprehend Indexing, Link building and everything else that's SEO you'll first need to comprehend how a search engine works. It's pretty easy but when you're working with 10000000000000s, yes 10000000000000s with a B. There are billions of sites and pages and it may get pretty perplexing.

I'll keep it easy. Let's get cracking, shall we? If you search for something on Google (once again, I'm going to say Google but I truly mean any search engine) you type it into "the box", called the "Search Bar".

Different individuals call the Search Bar assorted things. Like I said I'm going to keep it easy so to do so we'll continue referring to this box/bar as the Search Bar.

If you or anybody types anything into the Search Bar and pushes enter on the keyboard or clicks on submit with the mouse there's a lot of stuff happening that you'll never be able to see.

Working softly and rapidly behind the scenes Google scrubs its database of sites and pages and brings you the most relevant results. Much of the time. I'm not going to dig too deep into what precisely is going on as it's not truly crucial unless you're authoring a paper on the inner workings of Google.

Simply because you have a site on "sport fishing" for instance doesn't mean that when somebody searches for "sport fishing" they're going to arrive at your page. Chances are if you don't understand what you're doing no one really wants to view your page is going to discover it.

When Google discovers a page for you it's only going to discover the page/site if Google knows about it. Therefore how do you get Google to know about you and your site and or page and everything else you have to provide the Earth?

You're going to discover the answer as you read this. Remember you do need to know some basic background information on SEO in order to learn about Indexing and Link building.

Those are the 2 most crucial factors in your search engine success. First I'm going to go more into Indexing. When you comprehend that a bit more and really know how to go out and get in Google ASAP you'll be glad you understand all about Link building. Let's get moving on Indexing.

Chapter 2:
Intro to Indexing

Synopsis

Anytime you search for something on the net and acquire the results page for what you were searching, you're actually seeing part of the search engines Index. The SEO term for the results page or index page of a search engine is named the Search Engine Results Page or SERP. Let's look a bit farther into the Index and Indexing.

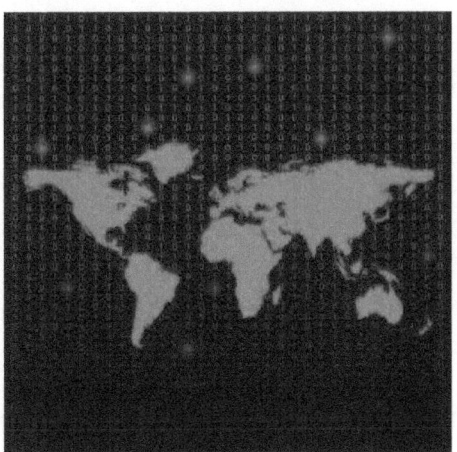

SERP

It's really pretty simple. Indexing kind of means what it sounds like. Consider a book, when you wish to find a particular part of page you typically view the Index as opposed to aimlessly flip-flopping through the pages attempting to find what you need. An Index is essentially a hierarchy of info.

When you're discussing a search engine it's pretty much the same matter. Except if you thought a 1,000 page book was a crazy amount to go through, conceive of a couple billion pages that may be searched in under a moment.

Google has an immense Index as I just stated. It's forever changing and growing but it's commonly looking through one hundred billion or so pages. So such as I was saying it truly is just a big book except you have to tell it what you require and not simply see what it has to pick from.

Indexing is the procedure of getting your page into Google's Index. I previously said that you don't get mechanically indexed in Google or any other search engine. Google is the most beneficial search engine to find info and for individuals to discover your info so it's great to be in there.

It doesn't care if you made the site(s) 2 minutes, months, and years of decades ago. A few of the older and other search engines won't even put you in the index till your page or site has been on the internet for at least a couple of months but commonly a couple of years.

On the other hand, Google's Index is constantly changing. What's raging one hour occasionally isn't so raging the next hour. Once again, this like anything else and is good and bad. You are able to search for something at 10 a.m. and it's # 1, you are able to then search for the precise same thing and discover that page has been moved down to # 89,823.

Google is all about relevancy and popularity. In numerous ways Search Engines are like adolescents. They highly value what others think and the more popular and "in" you are; the better you'll be handled.

I like to consider it like Day Trading and long-run investing on the securities market and other financial sectors. You are able to get your site in Google the same day you make it and it may be #1, for a day or for a year or eternally.

Yahoo on the other hand might take many months to get in but once you're in you are able to hold your rank pretty well. So again and finally, I'll just sum up what the Index of a search engine is and what Indexing is. The Index is what the search engine has already listed or indexed and Indexing is when you impart something to the Index or listing. Easy right?

Chapter 3:
What Your Page Needs For Indexing

Synopsis

While the basic idea of how the Index works is pretty simple, really getting Indexed may be a really difficult thing to accomplish, particularly if you're impatient. Explaining it is comparatively easy and that's what I am going to do. You are able to get into Google's index really simple and pretty quick if you play your cards right and abide by the "rules".

Get Your Page Ready

I ought to state now that I'm saying page and not site for a reason. Normally your whole web site consisting of lots of pages won't get indexed or at any rate it won't get indexed as a whole. It will be indexed page by page. You/individuals have assorted pages and links for a reason. Besides making it simple for your visitors to discover what they want, it makes it simple for Google to discover also. If you're decent to Google it'll be decent to you also.

The search engines have remote control computers named "spiders" or "bots". These spiders scrub the net for new or updated web pages. When they're out and about spidering or crawling (like a spider) they nearly always pick up on the fresh and or updated pages. In order for the spiders to crawl your page you'll simply need a couple of ingredients on your page.

Let's name the requirements to be indexed, indexing requirements all right? There are a few general requirements if you wish to Indexed. I'll go over them in detail and explain why every one is so crucial.

As an illustration, consider constructing a home. When you're constructing a home you don't simply have a home built in one day. You are able to likely do the foundation in a day with the correct team and tools however the furniture, fixtures, and so on... will take time.

Indexing Requirements

1. Page Title - a lot of individuals overlook this or really look too much into the title of your page. A great tip is to write for Google and not for

your viewers. There's a way to accomplish both but some view it as dishonorable, I'll get into this later.

The most crucial thing you truly need to pay attention to is that the title of your page coincides with the subjects of the page. Additionally it helps to have the word or phrase you wish to be indexed in Google in the literal title of your page. For instance, if you wish to get your page on auto detailing into Google you're going to need to have a title like "auto Detailing".

The title of your page is what partially tells Google what your page is about. Google is simply a computer so it simply understands so much. Keep it simple and you're all set. Incidentally, the
Title is part of what we call the "Meta" of "META" tags. Following, I'll get into those.

2. META Tags - You've likely heard of Meta Tags earlier. They're not so much for individuals as they are for the spiders or bots that search engines utilize when seeking info. They tell the search engines stuff that solely the search engines may see.

Tags:
I'm not certain how familiar you are with graffiti however when you see the writing on the walls, virtually, the spray paint on the outside of buildings or on overpasses or street sings, a few of those are called "tags". It's the people leaving there mark. You accomplish the same thing with your pages.

The definition for Meta is after or beyond. For us, this implies the extra parts of the page that we human beings don't require but that the spiders and bots require and wish to see after the viewer has

already seen the additional parts. A few individuals refer to Meta tags as "spider food" as the spiders that finally get you indexed adore these tags and it's like feeding the spiders. There are a lot of META tags, you truly only need to worry about 3 of them. All 3 are really crucial:

1. The Title Tag - I previously looked into this in the first part but simply to recap, this tag is where you wish to input the title of your page.

2. The Keyword Tag - once again, this ought to be self explanatory but the keyword tag is where you input your keywords for your page. The sole reason you pose keywords into the META tag area is so the search engines may see them so it recognizes what to do with your page.

3. The Description Tag - Like the additional tags, we don't do them to simply waste time, we do them to speak to the search engines in their own language. The description tag is where you put a description of the page you wish indexed.

A basic error with the description tag is to compose a description about your entire site. Unless you're working in the primary page or index page of your site this will be of no use to you or the search engines. If your page is on "PC speakers" you'll have to describe concisely what about PC speakers your page is about. Is it about how or where to purchase them or how they're made or? You get it...

The description tag is occasionally the sole tag that viewers may really see in the search engine listings. Not constantly but occasionally when searched correctly or when the page is pulled from the index in the correct way the surfer will see what your verbal description is.

Commonly the page is exhibited in the listing/index as a fast snippet of text from your page that the search engine believes will be of interest to the surfer based on what they wrote in the Search Box.

3. Page Content - once again, a few individuals will altogether overlook this part or again look into it a bit much. I stated previously that you need to attempt and write for Google and not for the real viewer. This holds true for particular aspects of your page and not for other parts. On the one hand when you're authoring for Google it may get you indexed rapidly and get you to appear high in the listings. On the other hand if you're writing to appeal simply to Google, it might leave the real viewer of the page in a haze and they'll simply leave.

The most beneficial way to approach material is to simply write enlightening, well laid out text and then go back and accent particular parts to make it SEO friendly. This essentially means simply making good utilization of your keywords throughout the material.

When I compose content I like to choose my keywords first. You're essentially targeting individuals who are seeking a very specific thing. In the long run you might get less traffic but you're getting a much more targeted or narrow audience which in spite of the name is a great thing.

Once you've the keywords you wish to utilize for the page you kind of just write around the keywords. The keywords are going to match your page with the keywords that individuals are searching for so make certain you do a little research.

4. The Page Layout and Design - If you view some of the most popular and long-familiar sites that you either heard about from an offline commercial or buzz or a net commercial or buzz what do you observe?

One thing that you ought to observe if you don't is that they're never too fancy and they're always simple to navigate. Again, this isn't only intended to make it simple for the viewer to get around and appealing to them visually but the HTML code that's utilized to build it is clean and easy.

Remember when I stated the spiders and robots that scrub the net are computers just like you're utilizing now. They don't care how fancy your page is. The clearer and simpler the code, the better.

A different design hint is to avoid too much CSS. CSS is an awesome way to get a head start on a design but keep everything to a minimal. The more basic HTML the better. Keeping it easy has never been simpler when you're utilizing simple HTML.

You don't need something that is so common and boring it looks like somebody who simply finished the 2d class of 5 in HTML design made it but you don't have to have anything too fancy or crazy. You'll discover that the sites of bands and musicians, and so forth... are commonly very heavy with graphics and flash and additional eye candy however they're commonly ranked very low in the Index.

The bots were made a long time ago and they still like the old school code and they'll repay you by getting you indexed quick and at a great position in the listings.

Please don't over think this or anything I've said too much. I'm merely giving you a few pointers. The best way to succeed with SEO is to try it out and see what works.

As I stated in earlier there's again a way to have a web site as fancy as you want with tons of artwork and extra codes, and so forth... that only viewers may see then another version for the bots that bears everything they want. I promise I'll go into that later.

By now you ought to have a pretty great grasp on the actual ingredients, elements, foundations or whatever else you wish to name them. You know the stuff you have to have to get your page indexed. But how do you really get indexed?

Chapter 4:
The Indexing Procedure

Synopsis

When you upload your page to your server you simply began the race to get indexed. Now, the search engines won't recognize you even uploaded anything for at least a couple of hours and in most cases a couple of days.

There are plenty of ways to get indexed nowadays and I'll go into those in a bit but here is what occurs from beginning to end when you get indexed.

What Happens

So as I was stating once you upload your page you've officially started the race.

The beginning part, is uploading your page. The bots are going to be seeking you if you did everything I stated. When they travel to your page they might not index you. They might put you in line to be indexed. Kind of like a provisional period.

You don't need to make any alterations to your page once you upload it so make certain it's the way you need it. Every time you update or alter the page, the bots know and will keep beginning from scratch with your page till it's indexed.

Even if it's already indexed and you make alterations it will come back to your page and update the search engine consequently which may be great and bad, so once again play it safe.

If you're not linked to a different site or vice versa the bots are going to discover you the difficult way. They're going to hit blocks of I.P. addresses (the virtual address of your site besides the .com part) and seek fresh pages and sites. The spiders that are doing the research will save your web site for export later to the Index.

You're vying with billions of additional sites occasionally all inside the same hour(s) to get indexed or get your page "crawled" by the spiders. So to review so far, once you upload your site it will sooner or later get crawled by the spiders/bots and it will either get indexed or included in line to be indexed.

You ought to make note that no web site is simply put in the Index immediately. It might get indexed but won't appear in the search results till the Index has been updated. No one knows when the official updates are but they occur every few hours or days.

You need the actual steps and tools you are able to use to make certain your page gets indexed. You are able to simply upload your page and it will sooner or later be indexed but that may take months or weeks and that's no fun.

As you'll soon discover, getting indexed may be pretty easy and materialize pretty quickly also. Just as easily and quickly as you get indexed, you are able to be De-Indexed or Banned. There's a difference between being De-Indexed and bluntly banned.

It's not a big difference but if you're banned your page and whole site are removed from the Index eternally. If your page gets De-Indexed it might just be one page from your web site or it might be the entire web site.

The difference is your page and or web site might be re-indexed, the chances are slight and it's nothing personal it's simply how it works. As we're talking mainly about Google, you ought to learn the Google SEO term "Sandbox" or "Sandboxed".

The Sandbox is what SEO people refer to the action of de-indexing or de-listing your page or whole site. The sites that get "Sandboxed" truly don't go anyplace, they simply don't come up in the search engine results for an indeterminate amount of time but for the most part you'll simply have to get the page(s) and or site(s) re-indexed utilizing the techniques you'll learn later.

O.K., your page is done and uploaded. Now comes the amusing part of going above and beyond the spiders and not awaiting them to come to you, but pressuring them to come to you.

Each technique of becoming indexed is simply a technique to get a back link. I'll explain in further detail what a back link is but simply remember back links are power in terms of indexing. So you'll comprehend this more soundly, let me discuss back links.

Back links are links from others to your page/site. Occasionally they're referred to as Incoming or Inbound links. These are similar to a popularity competition. The more links going to your Web site the better. Google and the search engines believe all these individuals like the web site so they're linking to it so we have to like it so we will index it.

Back links once again are solely useful if the individual who's linked to you is already indexed. You're simply leading the bots that on a regular basis visit these already indexed sites right to yours and you're accelerating the procedure.

Don't place all your eggs in one basket however. You are able to have zero links or back links and be #1 in the search engine for your Keyword(s). Back links are solely truly crucial when you are in a real competitive niche. In this case you should not be in such a popular niche, cash in on additional stuff.

There's millions of individuals in this country alone, everybody in the world may and does utilize the internet for the most part. Consider something and generally there's somebody wanting it. Utilize your marketing skills to make what you're offering worthy of individuals paying you for it.

Back links are essentially the idea behind each "technique" of getting indexed. There are simply different and immense ways to get back links and attention from the search engines. This is likely the most extended part of this whole subject and at the same time it's the most valuable.

Lastly back links are an awesome head start but not by a long sight are they the sole thing you ought to utilize to get indexed. If you can't achieve any back links in the next few sections I'll show you some other ways to get sites that are indexed to link to you.

Chapter 5:
From Google

Synopsis

Before we move into the next, more in-depth part of SEO, here are a few hints from Google themselves about other pages you need for your site which we haven't covered yet.

Extras You Need

Site Map

Place an HTML site map page on your web site, and utilize an XML Sitemap file.

A simple site map page with links to all of the pages or the most crucial pages (if you have 100s or 1000s) on your web site may be useful. Producing an XML Sitemap file for your site helps ensure that search engines find the pages on your web site. If you don't know how to create a sitemap, you are able to search it in Google for instructions.

Keep away from:

- letting your HTML site map page get out of date with broken links
- producing an HTML site map that merely lists pages without organizing them, for instance by subject

404 pages

Users will from time to time come to a page that doesn't exist on your web site, either by following a broken link or typing in the incorrect URL. Having a custom 404 page that kindly guides users back to a working page on your web site may greatly improve a user's experience.

Your 404 page ought to likely have a link back to your root page and may also provide links to popular or related material on your web site. Google provides a 404 widget that you will be able to embed in your 404 page to mechanically populate it with a lot of useful features. You are able to likewise use Google Webmaster Tools to discover the sources of URLs causing "not found" errors.

Keep away from:

- allowing your 404 pages to be indexed in search engines (make certain that your web server is configured to give a 404 HTTP status code when missing pages are requested)
- supplying only a vague message like "Not found", "404", or no 404 page at all
- utilizing a design for your 404 pages that isn't uniform with the rest of your web site.

Wrapping Up

Dedicate yourself to the process. SEO isn't a one-time event. Search engine algorithms alter on a regular basis, so the maneuvers that worked last year might not work this year. SEO calls for a long-term outlook and dedication.

Be patient. SEO isn't about blink of an eye gratification. Results frequently take months to see, and this is particularly true the smaller you are, and the newer you are to doing business online.

Make sure to check out the next book in this series for more in-depth ways to do SEO.

www.ingramcontent.com/pod-product-compliance
Lightning Source LLC
Chambersburg PA
CBHW030559220526
45463CB00007B/3119